LETTER ON THE DOUBLE ECLIPSE OF THE SUN

LETTER ON THE DOUBLE ECLIPSE OF THE SUN

DUNGAL OF BOBBIO

Copyright 2025 by Dalcassian Press

All rights reserved. No part of this book may be reproduced in any manner whatsoever without written permission except in the case of brief quotations embodied in critical articles and reviews.

No part of this publication may be reproduced, distributed, or transmitted in any form or by any means, including photocopying, recording, or other electronic or mechanical methods, without the prior written permission of the publisher, except in the case of brief quotations embodied in critical reviews and certain other non-commercial uses permitted by copyright law. For permission request, write to Dalcassian Press at admin@thescriptoriumproject.com

Translator: Curtin, D.P. (1985-)

ISBN: 979-8-3482-6893-0 (Paperback)
ISBN: 979-8-3482-6894-7 (eBook)
Library of Congress Control Number:

Printed by Ingram Content Group, 1 Ingram Blvd, La Vergne, Tennessee
First Printing 2025, Dalcassian Press, Wilmington, DE

This work is part of a series produced in association with the Scriptorium Project and its community of scholars and translators.
Please visit our website at: www.thescriptoriumproject.com

Letter on the Double Eclipse of the Sun

Translated by: D.P. Curtin

In the name of the Father, and of the Son, and of the Holy Spirit. To the most glorious Lord Charles, most serene Augustus, to all the noble and honorable princes of the Roman lineage, most studious in the gifts and exercises of royal virtues, long life, faithful health, continuous goodwill, peace, an unfading crown, and glory without end.

Therefore, I have heard, most beloved Lord, I, your faithful servant and orator Dungal, not forgetful that you sent a letter to Abbot Waldon, so that through it he might question me himself in your words about the reason for the eclipse of the sun, which you said had occurred twice last year from the incarnation of the Lord 810, and which, as you mentioned having read, not only ancient philosophers of the gentiles but also a certain bishop of Constantinople had previously described as a natural effect of the collision of elements, recognized through usual and certain expertise before it happened.

Hence, it seemed to your most blessed and most illustrious serenity to command that I, as a seeker of wisdom, should be asked what I thought, and what I knew, and what I would confess by expressing and responding. Therefore, I will not delay, nor will I conceal my response in accordance with your most holy and useful command; and would that I were as effective as I am willing, so that I could not only wish but also achieve what I desire, although before the highest Ruler, a humble and cheerful disposition is considered for the deed accomplished and fulfilled.

Since, therefore, my lord, the investigation and expertise of this matter pertains to philosophers, that is, to physicists properly and specifically, as your writings contain, whose more organized and diligent books, although they are not available to me, have treated these matters in a more practiced discourse and clearer expression, through which I believed I could respond to you more fully and learnedly about the inquiries. However, according to the simple and concise little books that are at hand, in as much as from them the dullness of a sluggish heart and slow sense can barely crawl and move with a slow effort, I shall respond, lest I seem to be repressed in a timid and stupid silence like the proverbial wolf in the tale. I know undoubtedly your most serene and most pious long-suffering indulgent clemency will easily grant me pardon if I say anything less or otherwise, and will modestly correct me with a paternal correction, as one who has erred through weakness and infirmity beyond my diligence or study.

However, the origin of this question must be revisited, so that from the beginning, as is customary in other discussions, the reasoning proceeds in order, and a suitable response is given to the inquiries. Therefore, Macrobius Ambrosius, in his exposition of Cicero, among other things, mentions the nine circles that surround it, that is, the largest sphere in which the twelve signs appear fixed, and to which seven other spheres are subjected through which the two lights, the sun and the moon, and the five wandering stars move. Of these orbs, that is, of the aforementioned circles, the first is the galactic circle, which is interpreted in Latin as milky, which alone is subject to the eyes, while the other circles are understood more by thought than by sight. The second is the zodiacal circle, that is, the sign-bearing one, called so for carrying and containing the signs, that is, the stars and constellations. The other five circles are called parallels, named so because they are neither all equal nor unequal; of which Virgil mentions in the Georgics.

Besides these, there are two others called Colures, which were named due to imperfect conversion: the two that are added to the aforementioned number, the Meridian and the Horizon, are not written in the sphere because they cannot have a fixed place, but vary according to the diversity of the observer or the inhabitant. All these things, named and numbered transitively, do not need to be explained in this context. Therefore, the aforementioned two lights, that is, the sun and the moon, and the five stars that are called wandering, have divided the seven mentioned spheres, subject to the largest sphere containing the twelve signs, which is called the zodiac, and each has obtained its own and special inheritances in the occupied regions.

In the first sphere, there is the star called Saturn, in the second Jupiter, in the third Mars, in the fourth, which is the middle, the sun, in the fifth the star of Venus, in the sixth Mercury; the seventh, which is the outermost and lowest of all, is held by the moon. Thus Cicero describes, to whom Archimedes and the reasoning of the Chaldeans agree. Plato, however, confirms that above the moon, in the sixth place among the seven, the sun holds its position, following the Egyptians, the parents of all philosophical disciplines, who wish for the sun to be located between the moon and Mercury. Although this belief of Cicero and his authors has gained strength, supported by certain edicts and credible reasons, and has been accepted by almost all for use, the more insightful observation of Plato seems to have discovered a truer order, which, apart from visual investigation, is also recommended by this reasoning: that the moon, which lacks its own light and borrows from the sun, must necessarily be subject to the source of its light; for this reasoning makes the moon not to have its own light, while all other stars shine with their own, since they are located above the sun in the very purest ether, in which everything that exists, to speak in the words of the Philosopher, is natural light and its own, which together with its own fire so encroaches upon the sphere of the sun that the zones of the heavens, which are far from the sun, are perpetually oppressed by cold; but the moon, because it is alone under the sun and close to the region of the perishable, which lacks its own light, could not shine. Finally, since the lowest part of the whole world is the earth, and the lowest part of the ether is the moon, and they called the moon the earth but ethereal, it could not be immobile like the earth, because in the sphere that revolves, nothing remains immobile except the center; however, the earth is the center of the mundane sphere, therefore it alone remains immobile: again, the earth, having received the light of the sun, shines only, it does not emit light; the moon emits light like a mirror, which, although it is a denser body than the other celestial bodies, is, however, much purer than the earthly, becoming permeable to the received light, so that it emits it again from itself, yet without conveying any sense of heat to us, because the ray of light, when it reaches us from its origin, that is, from the sun, carries with it the nature of the fire from which it is born; but when it is infused into the body of the moon, and shines from there, it reflects only brightness, not heat: for even a mirror, when it sends forth brightness from itself, shows only the likeness of fire without the sensation of heat.

It should be added that, besides the sun and the moon, and the five stars which are called wandering, all the other stars are fixed in the sky, and can only move with the sky. Others, whose assertion is closer to the truth, have also said that these move by their own motion, besides being carried along with the conversion of the sky, but due to the immensity of the outermost sphere, they are believed to consume a credible number of ages in one course of their ambition, and therefore none of their motion can be perceived by humans; since the span of human life is not sufficient even for a brief moment to detect such a slow approach. However, the sun and the moon and the five stars, which are misnamed due to their wandering, besides the daily conversion of the sky that they drag along from rise to set, are proven to move by their own motion eastward from the west, leading to arguments that point to the truth, for both sight and reason affirm that they are not fixed to the sky, while they are seen now in this region of the sky, now in that, and often when two or more have gathered into one, they separate from the place where they were seen together and from each other afterwards, which fixed stars do not do, but they are always seen in the same places, nor do they ever disperse from their union, while they are seen to revolve from rise to set in a contrary motion not only by the most manifest reasoning but also by approving eyes.

For indeed, considering the order of the signs by which we see the zodiac divided or distinguished, I will take the beginning from any one sign of its order: when Aries rises, Taurus emerges after it; the Twins follow this, then Cancer, and the rest in order. Therefore, if these were to proceed westward from the east, they would not turn from Aries to Taurus, which is placed behind, nor from Taurus to the later sign of Gemini: but they would proceed in a straight and harmonious motion from Gemini to Taurus, and from Taurus to Aries. However, since they revolve from the first sign to the second, from the second to the third, and then to the remaining later ones, and the fixed signs are borne in the sky, it is undoubtedly clear that these stars move not with the sky, but against it. To make this fully clear, I will assert regarding the course of the moon, which is notable both for its brightness and speed. It is seen around sunset on the second day, and as if close to the sun, which it has recently left, it holds the edge of the sky preceding the west; on the third day, it sets later than on the second; and thus it recedes further from sunset each day, so that on the seventh day, around sunset, it appears in the middle of the sky, while after another seven days when the sun sets, it rises, measuring half the sky, that is, one hemisphere, by receding from west to east; again after another seven days, it holds the peak of the hidden hemisphere around sunset, the indication of which is that it rises at midnight: finally, after the same number of days has passed, plus or minus another two, it again catches the sun, and both appear to rise together, as long as it moves succeeding the sun, and again receding, it always gradually leaves the sunset to the east. The sun itself also moves in no other way than from sunset to east, and again receding, it always gradually leaves the sunset to the east; the sun itself naturally moves from sunset to east. And although it recedes more slowly than the moon, since it occupies one sign for as long as the moon travels through the entire zodiac, it nevertheless provides clear and visible indications of its motion: I will place it in Aries, which, being an equinoctial sign, makes equal hours of sleep and day. In this sign, when it sets, we soon see Libra, that is, the claws of Scorpio rising, and Taurus appears near the sunset: for we see the brighter parts of Taurus, the Pleiades and Hyades, shortly after the sun sets. In the following month, the sun recedes into the later sign, that is, into Taurus, and thus it happens that neither the Pleiades nor any other part of Taurus is seen that month: for the sign that sets with the sun is always hidden, so much so that even the nearby stars are concealed by the proximity of the sun: for even Canis, since it is near Taurus, is not seen, covered by the proximity of the light. And this is what Virgil says: "The white bull opens the year with golden horns, and the dog sets with the opposing star." It is not intended to be understood that the dog is made to set with the sun when Taurus rises, but he said it sets while Taurus carries the sun, because then it begins not to be seen, being close to the sun. However, when the sun sets, Libra is found so high that the whole of Scorpio appears risen; the Twins, however, are seen near sunset; again after the month of Taurus, the Twins are not seen, which signifies that the sun has migrated from them. After the Twins, it returns to Cancer, and then when it sets, Libra is soon seen in the middle of the sky: thus it is clear that the sun has receded through three signs, that is, Aries, Taurus, and Gemini to the middle of the hemisphere.

Finally, after the next three months, with the three signs that follow, Cancer, Leo, and Virgo, it is found in Libra; which again equalizes the night with the day, and while it sets in that sign, Aries soon rises, in which the sun used to set six months before. Therefore, we have chosen to prioritize its setting over its rising, because the later signs are seen after sunset, and while they are usually seen when the sun sets, we show the sun returning, undoubtedly indicating that it recedes with contrary motion to how the sky moves. Moreover, what we have said about the sun and the moon is also sufficient to assign the recess of the five stars: for by the same reasoning, migrating to the later signs, they are always involved in a contrary recession to the mundane motion, the courses and returns of which are said to be regulated by the sun itself; for there is a certain definition of space, to which when each erratic star, receding, has reached the sun, it seems to be prohibited from going further, and appears to move backward, and when it has reached a certain part in receding, it is recalled to its usual direct course, thus the power and influence of the sun's motion governs the movement of the other lights established by definite measurement.

The circle, or circus, is understood as the complete and finished revolution of each star, that is, a return to the same place after traversing the sphere through which it moves. This is the line surrounding the sphere, creating a path along which the sun and moon travel, and within which the legitimate wandering of the stars is constrained, which is why the ancients said they err, because they are carried in their course, and against the motion of the greatest sphere, that is, the heavens, they are rolled in the opposite direction from west to east, and indeed all have equal speed, similar motion, the same manner of moving, but not all complete their circles in the same period of time. The cause of this inequality of space under the same speed is the different distances of the spheres that each star traverses: from the sphere of Saturn, which is the first of seven, to the sphere of Jupiter, the distance of the second intervening space is such that the upper zodiacal circle is completed in thirty years, while the twelve below it is completed in twelve; again, the sphere of Mars recedes from Jupiter by such a distance that it completes the same course in two years. Venus, however, is so much lower than the region of Mars that a year is sufficient for it to traverse the zodiac. Now indeed, the star Mercury is so close to Venus, and the sun is close to Mercury, that these three traverse their heavens in approximately the same period of time, that is, in a year plus or minus; therefore Cicero called these two courses companions of the sun, because they never recede far from it in equal time: the moon, however, has receded so much downward from these that it completes what they do in a year in twenty-eight days. But Cicero, when he wishes to refer to the fourth of the seven, states that the fourth is not nearly the middle among the seven, but is indeed both the middle and is regarded as such; he did not abruptly call the sun the middle, but rather nearly the middle with these words: "Then of the seven, the sun occupies the middle region." But the addition of this statement is not without qualification; for the sun, occupying the fourth place, holds the middle region in number, but not in space; for the star of Saturn, which is the highest, traverses the zodiac in thirty years: the sun in one year; the moon last in one incomplete month. Therefore, there is as much difference between the sun and Saturn as between one and thirty; as much between the moon and the sun as between twelve and one; hence it is clear that no certain division of the whole space from the highest to the lowest is made in the region of the sun. But as far as number is concerned, just as the fourth is called the middle among seven, although due to the inequality of spaces the addition is nearly qualified. Therefore, the zodiac is one circle out of the eleven aforementioned, which alone could obtain latitude in the manner we refer to. The nature of celestial circles is incorporeal, and the line is conceived in such a way that it is considered to have only length, and cannot have width; in the zodiac, the length of the signs requires capacity. Therefore, as much space as the wide dimension occupies with the extended stars, it is limited by two lines, and a third drawn through the middle is called the ecliptic, because when both the sun and moon complete their course along the same line, it is necessary for one of them to experience an eclipse; of the sun, if the moon succeeds it; of the moon, if it is then opposite the sun. Therefore, the sun never suffers an eclipse, except when it is the thirtieth day of the moon; and the moon does not know an eclipse on the fifteenth day of its course: for it happens that either the moon, positioned opposite the sun, obstructs solid light by the conical shadow of the earth found along the same line, or the sun, when the moon succeeds it, repels its light from human sight by its projection. In an eclipse, however, the sun itself suffers nothing, but our sight is deprived, while the moon labors around its own eclipse, not receiving the light of the sun, by whose benefit it colors the night; knowing this, Virgil, the most learned in all disciplines, said: "The various eclipses of the sun, and the labors of the moon." Therefore, although the paths of the three lines both close and divide the zodiac, nevertheless, antiquity wished to call it one circle, according to certain philosophers, the width of the zodiac is measured by twelve lines, of which, according to the nature of equal numbers, it is necessary to have two middle ones, which are confirmed to be illuminated solely by the sun, while they say the moon travels through all. Therefore, it does not allow an eclipse to happen wandering back and forth each month. Nevertheless, in all years, they confirm that the eclipses of both stars occur on set days and hours, although they do not always appear, because sometimes they occur below the earth in the part of the hidden hemisphere, sometimes above; but due to clouds and the globularity and convexity of the earth, they can neither be seen everywhere nor at the same hours by all; hence it is most certain that these happen more often than they are seen, nor do they appear equally to all when they are seen; hence the eastern eclipses of the sun and moon are not felt, nor the western morning ones, the cone of the earth and the obstructing sight intervening. However, the eclipse of the moon sometimes occurs five months earlier, while that of the sun is seen twice in thirty days above the earth, and we have learned from others that both stars have been seen to eclipse on certain occasions within twelve days, based on plausible reasoning and tradition.

I replied, therefore, as it seems to me, most blessed Augustus, according to your demand for letters, and I spoke from their authority regarding how the ancient philosophers both knew and foresaw how the eclipse of the sun would occur, and when it would happen. For they were the most skilled in all disciplines, and unaware of none of the ancient approved sects, with the most acute and clarified intention of their purified minds, and with the most perspicuous and thoroughly purified sight of their internal senses fixed upon it, they sought with the utmost subtlety and urgency the natures, reasons, causes, and origins of all things through natural investigation. They discovered, found, and diligently and intently observed what was sought, from him from whom every good gift is given and every perfect gift is offered. Thus, the physicists, especially those studying astronomy, with the same prolonged and meditative diligence, gazing at the rising and setting of the stars, fully explored the courses and returns of the sun, moon, and the other five wandering stars, to such an extent that through their exploration they knew without a doubt how many degrees of the zodiac each wandering star would traverse, and how it would specifically and particularly direct its course along those degrees, and in which sign and in which part of that sign it would be. Therefore, those who so certainly and studiously understood the more subtle, albeit true and natural, movements of the other stars, why did they not know the courses of the sun and moon, which are indeed more notable and easier to understand, so that they were unaware of how or when they would travel along the same ecliptic line of the zodiac, and traversing that one and the same line, would converge into one sign and one part, and coming together in the same part, an eclipse of the sun would occur when the moon succeeded the sun.

Therefore, the aforementioned philosophers not only foresaw the eclipse, that is, the defect of the sun, and knowing it, predicted when it would occur after one month; but also when it would follow after a year, or twenty or a hundred years, they would long before have experienced it through that aforementioned keen exploration and diligent observation. But to make you marvel even more, they extended such arguments up to fifteen thousand years. Hence, Cicero, referring to the vision of Africanus, says: "People commonly measure the year only by the return of one star, the sun; but in truth, when all the stars have returned to the same place from which they once set out, and have brought back the same description of the whole sky at long intervals: then that can truly be called a turning year, in which I hardly dare to say how many generations of men are contained. For as once the sun seemed to fail and be extinguished for men, when the spirit of Romulus penetrated into these very temples, whenever the sun would again fail from the same part and at the same time, then, with all signs recalled to the same beginning, consider the year completed; of which year know that not even a twentieth part has yet turned."

These words of Cicero are thus opened and explained by the Ambrosian expression: The year is not just that which the common usage now calls; but for each of the luminaries, that is, the sun and the moon, or the stars, the year is their own: thus, the lunar month is the year within which it traverses the orbit of the sky; for it is called a month from the moon, because in Greek the moon is called μήνη.

Finally, Virgil, wishing to signify the lunar year, which is short, as compared to the year which is made by the course of the sun, says: "Meanwhile, the great sun revolves around the year." Calling it a great year in comparison to the lunar; for indeed the courses of Venus and Mercury are nearly equal to the sun; however, the year of Mars holds nearly two years: for in such a time it circuits the sky. The star of Jupiter, however, consumes twelve years, and that of Saturn thirty years in the same circuit.

These things about the sun and moon, and the wandering stars, as we have previously recounted, are now known: but the year which is called mundane, which is truly turning, because it is made by the full conversion of the universe, is explained by the most abundant centuries, the ratio of which is as follows. All stars and celestial bodies, which are fixed in the sky and whose proper motion human sight can never feel or perceive, are nevertheless moved, and besides the whirling of the heavens to which they are always drawn, they also advance with their own approach so slowly that no human life is so long that it can observe continuously made from the place of change, in which [...] it first saw, and perceive. Therefore, the end of the mundane year is when all stars and all celestial bodies, which it has as wandering, have returned from a certain place to the same place in such a way that not even one star in the sky is in another place than it was, when all the others have moved from that place to which they returned, they have given an end to their year, so that the sun and moon with the five wandering stars are in the same places and parts in which they were at the beginning of the mundane year: this, as the physicists wish, occurs after fifteen thousand years have passed.

Therefore, just as the year of the moon is a month, and the year of the sun consists of twelve months, and these are the years of other stars that we have mentioned above; so the mundane year amounts to fifteen thousand years, as we currently calculate. That year, therefore, is truly called a turning year, which is not measured by the return of the sun, that is, one star, but by the return of all the stars that are in any sky to the same place under the same description of the whole sky; hence it is called mundane, because the world is properly called the sky. Thus, just as we call the year of the sun not only from the Kalends of January to the same, but also from the following day after the Kalends to the same day, and from any day of any month to the same day, it is called a year; so each person makes the beginning of this mundane year whatever he decides, as for example now Cicero established for himself the beginning of the mundane year from the eclipse of the sun that occurred at the end of Romulus, and although many eclipses of the sun have happened afterwards, it is not said that the mundane year was fulfilled by the repeated eclipse of the sun, but it will be fulfilled when the sun, being eclipsed, will be in the same places and parts, and will find all the stars of the sky and all the constellations again in the positions they were under Romulus, when after fifteen thousand years, as philosophers assert, the sun will again be eclipsed in such a way that it will be in the same sign and the same part, at the same beginning in which they were under Romulus, with all the stars and signs recalled.

Therefore, in the year 810 from the incarnation of the Lord, it is not surprising that an eclipse of the sun occurred, as your letters indicate; on the seventh of the Ides of June, with the first moon beginning, and again in the same year on the day before the Kalends of December, with the thirtieth moon beginning, and from the prior eclipse in the seventh month, that is, starting in December; which eclipse of the sun is defined to occur at the last of the first moon, and in the seventh month from the prior eclipse, although sometimes it does not appear at all, since it has certainly occurred, or if it has appeared, it is not always seen everywhere, or if it is seen everywhere, not all see it equally at the same hours due to the aforementioned causes.

If anyone, therefore, even at this time, endowed with such sharpness of sense, striving with such long-lasting urgency, intent on such diligence of exploration and observation, applies the same idleness and curiosity as those born in the earlier age, is it not easy to believe that he can reach the same ancient knowledge and foresight? For it is the disparate will, not nature, which is one and equal, that makes men distant from each other, although we have found that in the first men, due to the youth of the world and the force of bodies, and the vigor of the senses, they seemed to desire more.

Here, therefore, let the discourse on the eclipse of the sun come to an end, not because I think I have perhaps said enough, but because at present the limitations of my own ability do not allow me to elaborate further: for Pliny the Elder and other books, through which I think I can supplement this, are not available to us in these parts, since I dare not conceive anything on such matters by myself nor presume to do so. But you, most pious Lord Augustus, to whom God has distributed the abundance of wisdom above all, as well as other holy virtues, I humbly ask that in whatever way I seem to be ignorant about this matter, or to estimate it otherwise than is right, you may be pleased to instruct and direct me: For God has chosen the foolish things of the world: And, There is no acceptance of persons with him, so that not only may the light of your purest and brightest wisdom shine upon those who are near, but also upon those who are far; and not only may it illuminate those running through the open fields, but also may it pour over the secluded through the cracks and joints of your most serene radiance. Therefore, it is very necessary for all to pray and beseech with attentive and constant prayers, that the Lord and Savior Jesus Christ may grant and bestow upon his people to rejoice for many years in such a great prince and teacher, who is the principal teacher of all good works and virtues and honorable disciplines, and is held as the perfect example for rulers to govern their subjects well, for soldiers to exercise their legitimate military service, for clerics to rightly observe the rites of universal Christian religion, for philosophers and scholars to philosophize and gain wisdom honorably about human matters, and to reverently and orthodoxly think and believe about divine matters. What more can I strive to say about the supreme virtues and excellences of our Lord Augustus Charles, since although I would like to elaborate much, I will not be able to recount everything? This only we truly say, that all with one voice proclaim, that in this land, where the Franks now dominate by God's grace, such a king and such a prince has never been seen since the beginning of the world, who is so strong, wise, and religious as our Lord Augustus Charles. Furthermore, through his holy and sublime merits, perhaps from his seed such a one may arise. It remains for us all, as Christians, to cry out with the highest voices and most devoted hearts unanimously to the Lord and ask that he multiply the triumphs of our most excellent Lord Augustus Charles, extend his empire, preserve the sacred progeny, confirm health, and prolong life in the many years of its course. Hear, hear, hear, O Christ.

Therefore, as you, most reverend and sweetest lord, have commanded your faithful servant Waldon the abbot to question me by reminding me of such things from your words, and to demand from me, who, as faithful to you, has been a serious and importunate collector of this matter, although he has been moderate, I therefore send him back to you, that you may give him thanks if I have said anything good in these matters, which I, willingly or unwillingly, have paid due to his urgent demand; but if I have said anything wrong due to my own negligence, may you kindly impose upon me whatever penance you wish. I wish you always to be well in God, most excellent lord, and not only most excellent lord, but also most pious and most loving Father.

Latin Text

Epistola de duplici solis eclipsi anno 810

In nomine Patris, et Filii, et Spiritus sancti. Domino gloriosissimo Carolo serenissimo Augusto, omnium antecedentium Romanorum principum cunctis nobilibus honestisque regalium virtutum donis et exercitiis studiosissimo, vita longaeva, fida salus, continua benevolentia, pax, corona immarcescibilis, gloria sine fine.

Audivi ergo, Domine dilectissime, ego Dungal vester fidelis famulus et orator, non immemor quod vos Waldoni abbati direxistis epistolam, ut per illam me ipse ex vestris verbis interrogaret de ratione defectus solis, quem anno praeterito ab incarnatione Domini 810 bis evenisse plurium relatu vobis fuisse compertum dixistis, et quem sicut vos legisse memorastis, non solum antiqui gentilium philosophi, sed et quidam Constantinopolitanus episcopus, quasi naturalem concursionis elementorum effectum usitatae et certae explorationis peritia cognitum prius dixere, quam fieret.

Inde vestrae beatissimae et clarissimae serenitati visum est mandare ut de dicta causa ego quasi sector sapientiae interrogarer quid sentirem, et quid scirem, et quid sentirem proferendo et respondendo faterer, exceptum scriberetur, scriptumque vobis deferretur. Non differam igitur, neque dissimulabo vestro secundum vires sanctissimo et utilissimo parere praecepto; et utinam tam efficax quam voluntarius existerem, ut non solum velle, sed et compote voto assequi cupita valerem, licet apud summum Rectorem pronus et alacris affectus pro re effecta et adimpleta reputatur.

Quia ergo, domine mi, hujus rationis investigatio et peritia ad philosophos, hoc est, physicos proprie et specialiter pertinet, sicut vestri continent apices, quorum libri compositiores et diligentiores quamvis mihi non suppetant, quibus de his rebus et de talibus exercitatiori sermone et enucleatiori expressione tractaverunt, et per quos vobis plenius et eruditius de inquisitis respondere me posse crediderim. Secundum simplices tamen et leves compendiososque libellos qui inter manus sunt, in quantum de ipsis torpor obtunsi cordis et tardus sensus vix lento conamine pigroque nisu reptans et movens, praelibare quiverit, ne vulgari proverbio lupus in fabula, pavido stupidoque silentio reprimi videar, utcunque respondebo; sciens indubitatissime vestram serenissimae et piissimae longanimitatis indulgibilem clementiam, si quid minus aut aliter dixero, facilem mihi veniam donaturam, et paterna correctione me veluti praeter industriam studiumve per fragilitatem infirmitatemque delinquentem modeste castigaturam.

Hujus autem quaestionis origo repetenda est, ut ab initio sicut in caeteris solet disputationibus, per ordinem ratio explicanda procedens, congrua reddatur de interrogatis responsio. Macrobius igitur Ambrosius in expositione Ciceronis inter caetera commemorat de novem circulis, qui aplanen illam ambiunt, hoc est maximam sphaeram in qua duodecim signa videntur infixa, et cui subjectae septem aliae sphaerae per quas duo lumina sol et luna et vaga quinque discurrunt. Orbium autem, hoc est circulorum praedictorum, primus est galactias, quod latine lacteus interpretatur, qui solus subjacet oculis, caeteris circulis magis cogitatione quam visu comprehendendis. Secundus zodiacus circulus, hoc est signifer, signa, id est, stellas et sidera ferendo et continendo dictus. Quinque alii circuli parelleli vocantur, dicti hoc nomine, quod neque in omnibus aequales sunt, neque inaequales; de quibus Virgilius memorat in Georgicis.

Praeter hos alii duo sunt Coluri quibus nomen dedit imperfecta conversio: duo, qui numero praedicto superadduntur, Meridianus et Horizon non scribuntur in sphaera, quia certum locum habere non possunt, sed pro diversitate circumspicientis habitantisve variantur:

quae omnia transitive nominata et numerata in hoc loco non est opus exponere. Duo ergo praedicta lumina, hoc est sol et luna, et quinque stellae quae appellantur vagae, septem memoratas sphaeras maximae sphaerae duodecim signa continenti, quae aplanes vocatur, subjectas dispertiverunt, et occupatis regionibus quasi proprias et speciales haereditates singulae singulas obtinuerunt.

In prima autem sphaera de septem illa est stella quae dicitur Saturni, in secunda Jovis, in tertia Martis, in quarta hoc est media, sol, in quinta stella Veneris, in sexta Mercurii; septimam quae est omnium extima et infima, luna tenet. Ita Cicero describit, cui Archimedes et Chaldaeorum ratio consentit. Plato vero a luna sursum secundum, hoc est, inter septem a summo locum sextum solem tenere confirmat, secutus Aegyptios omnium philosophiae disciplinarum parentes, qui ita solem inter lunam et Mercurium locatum volunt. Quamvis autem ista persuasio Tullii et auctorum ejus quibusdam edictis et credibilibus rationibus fulta convaluit, et ab omnibus pene in usum recepta est, perspicacior tamen Platonis observatio veriorem ordinem deprehendisse videtur, quam praeter indaginem visus haec quoque ratio commendat, quod lunam quae luce propria caret, et de sole mutuatur, necesse est fonti luminis sui esse subjectam; haec enim ratio lunam facit non habere lumen proprium, caeteras omnes stellas lucere suo, quod illae supra solem locatae in ipso purissimo aethere sunt, in quo omne quidquid est, ut verbis Philosophi loquar, lux naturalis et sua est, quae tota cum igne suo ita sphaerae solis incumbit, ut coeli zonae quae procul a sole sunt perpetuo frigore oppressae sint; luna vero, quia ipsa sola sub sole est, et caducorum jam regioni luce sua carenti proxima, lucere non potuit. Denique quia totius mundi ima pars terra est, aetheris autem ima pars luna est, lunam autem terram sed aetheream vocaverunt, immobilis autem ut terra esse non potuit, quia in sphaera quae volvitur nihil manet immobile praeter centrum; mundanae autem sphaerae terra centrum est, ideo sola immobilis perseverat: rursus terra accepto solis lumine clarescit tantummodo, non lucet; luna speculi instar lumen quo illustratur emittit, quae quamvis densius corpus sit quam caetera coelestia, ut multum tamen terreno purius, fit acceptae luci penetrabile, adeo ut eam de se rursus emittat, nullum tamen ad nos praeferentem sensum caloris, quia lucis radius cum ad nos de origine sua, id est, de sole pervenit, naturam secum ignis de quo nascitur devehit; cum vero in lunae corpus infunditur, et inde resplendet, solam refundit claritudinem, non calorem: nam et speculum cum splendorem de se vi oppositi eminus ignis immittit, solam ignis similitudinem carentem sensu caloris ostendit.

His illud adjiciendum est, praeter solem et lunam, et stellas quinque quae appellantur vagae, reliquas omnes alias infixas coelo, nec nisi cum coelo moveri. Alii, quorum assertio vero propior est, has quoque dixerunt suo motu, praeter quod cum coeli conversione feruntur, accedere, sed propter immensitatem extimi globi excedentia credibilem numerum saecula multa una cursus sui ambitione consumere, et ideo nullum earum motum ab homine sentiri; cum non sufficiat humanae vitae spatium ad breve saltem punctum tam tardae accessionis deprehendendum. Solem autem ac lunam et stellas quinque, quibus ab errore nomen, praeter quod secum trahit ab ortu in occasum coeli diurna conversio, ipsa suo motu in orientem ab occidente procedere, argumentis ad verum ducentibus comprobatur, moveri enim coeloque non esse infixas et visus et ratio affirmat, dum modo in hac, modo in illa coeli regione visuntur, et saepe cum in unum duae pluresve convenerint, et a loco in quo simul visae sunt, et a se postea separantur, quod infixae stellae non faciunt, sed in iisdem locis semper videntur, nec a sui unquam se copulatione dispergunt, ab ortu vero ad occasum in contrarium motu propiore volvi non solum manifestissima ratione, sed oculis quoque approbantibus demonstratur.

Considerato enim signorum ordine, quibus zodiacum divisum vel distinctum videmus, ab uno signo quolibet ordinis ejus sumam exordium: cum Aries exoritur, post ipsum Taurus emergit; hunc Gemini sequuntur, hos Cancer, et per ordinem reliqua. Si istae ergo in occidentem ab oriente procederent, non ab Ariete in Taurum, qui retro locatus est, nec a Tauro in Geminos signum posterius volverentur: sed a Geminis in Taurum, et a Tauro in Arietem rectae et mundanae volubilitatis consona accessione procederent. Cum vero a primo signo in secundum, a secundo ad tertium, et inde ad reliqua quae posteriora sunt revolvuntur, signa autem infixa coelo feruntur, sine dubio constat has stellas non cum coelo, sed contra coelum moveri. Hoc ut plene luceat, astruam de lunae cursu, quae et claritate sua et velocitate notabilior est. Secundo fere die circa occasum videtur, et quasi vicina soli, quem nuper reliquit, postquam ille demersus est, ipsa coeli marginem tenet antecedenti super occidens; tertio die tardius occidit quam secundo; et ita quotidie longius ab occasu recedit, ut septimo die circa solis occasum in medio coelo ipsa videatur, post alios vero septem cum ille mergit, haec oritur, adeo media parte mensis dimidium coelum, id est, unum hemisphaerium ab occasu in orientem recedendo metitur; rursus post septem alios circa solis occasum latentis hemisphaerii verticem tenet, cujus rei indicium est quod medio noctis exoritur: postremo totidem diebus exactis, additis insuper plus minusve aliis duobus, solem denuo comprehendit, et vicinus videtur ortus amborum, quandiu soli succedens rursus moveatur, et rursus recedens paulatim semper in orientem regrediendo relinquat occasum. Sol quoque ipse non aliter quam ab occasu in orientem movetur, et rursus recedens paulatim semper in orientem regrediendo relinquit occasum; sol quoque ipse naturaliter quam ab occasu in orientem movetur. Et licet tardius recessum suum quam luna conficiat, quippe quod tanto tempore signum unum emetiatur quanto totum zodiacum luna discurrit, manifesta tamen et subjecta oculis motus sui praestat indicia: hunc enim in Ariete esse ponam, quod quia aequinoctiale signum est, pares horas somni et diei facit. In hoc signo cum occidit, Libram, id est, Scorpii chelas mox oriri videmus, et apparet Taurus vicinus occasui: nam Vergilias et Hyadas partes Tauri clariores non multo post solem mergentes videmus. Sequenti mense sol in signum posterius, id est in Taurum recedit, et ita fit ut neque Vergiliae, neque alia pars Tauri illo mense videatur: signum enim quod et cum sole occidit, semper occulitur, adeo ut et vicina astra solis propinquitate celentur: nam et

Canis tunc, quia vicinus Tauro est, non videtur, tectus lucis propinquitate. Et hoc est quod Virgilius ait: Candidus auratis aperit eum cornibus annum Taurus, et adverso cedens Canis occidit astro. Non enim vult intelligi Tauro oriente cum sole mox in occasu fieri Canem, qui proximus Tauro est, sed occidere eum dixit Tauro gestante solem, quia tunc incipit non videri, sole vicino. Tunc tamen occidente sole Libra adeo superior invenitur, ut totus Scorpius ortus appareat; Gemini vero vicini tunc videntur occasui; rursus post Tauri mensem Gemini non videntur, quod in eos solem migrasse significat. Post Geminos redit in Cancrum, et tum cum occidit mox Libra in medio coelo videtur: adeo constat solem tribus signis peractis, id est, Ariete et Tauro et Geminis ad medietatem hemisphaerii recessisse.

Denique post tres menses sequentes, tribus signis quae sequuntur incensis, Cancrum dico, Leonem et Virginem, invenitur in Libra; quae rursus aequat noctem diei, et dum in ipso signo occidit, mox oritur Aries, in quo sol ante sex menses occidere solebat. Ideo autem occasum ejus quam ortum elegimus praeponendum, quia signa posteriora post occasum videntur, et dum ad haec quo sole mergente videri solent, solem redire monstramus, sine dubio eum contrario motu recedere quam coelum movetur, ostendimus. Haec autem quae de sole ac luna diximus, etiam quinque stellarum recessum assignare sufficient: pari enim ratione in posteriora signa migrando, semper mundanae volubilitati contraria recessione versantur, quarum cursus recursusque ipso sole moderari perhibetur; nam certa spatii definitio est, ad quam cum unaquaeque erratica stella recedens ad solem pervenerit, tanquam ultra prohibeatur accedere, agi retro videtur et rursus cum certam partem recedendo contigerit, ad directi cursus consueta revocatur, ita solis vis et potestas motus reliquorum luminum constituta demensione moderatur.

Circus ergo sive circulus intelligitur uniuscujusque stellae una integra et peracta conversio, id est, ab eodem loco post emensum sphaerae per quam movetur ambitum in eumdem locum regressus. Est autem hic linea ambiens sphaeram ac veluti semitam faciens, per quam sol et luna discurrit, et intra quam vagantium stellarum error legitimus coercetur, quas ideo veteres errare dixerunt, quia et cursu suo feruntur, et contra sphaerae maximae, id est, ipsius coeli impetum contrario motu ad orientem ab occidente volvuntur, et omnium quidem par celeritas, motus similis, idem est modus meandi, sed non omnes eodem temporis spatio circos suos orbesque conficiunt. Causam vero sub eadem celeritate diversi spatii inaequalitas sphaerarum efficit, quas singulae stellae perlustrant: a Saturni enim sphaera, quae est prima de septem, usque ad sphaeram Jovis, a summo secundam interjecti spatii tanta distantia est, ut zodiaci ambitum superior triginta annis, duodecim vero subjecta conficiat, rursus tantum a Jove sphaera Martis recedit, ut eumdem cursum biennio peragat. Venus autem tanto est a regione Martis inferior, ut ei annus satis sit ad zodiacum peragrandum.

Jam vero ita Veneri proxima est stella Mercurii, et Mercurio sol propinquus, ut hi tres coelum suum pari temporis spatio, id est, anno plus minusve circumeant; ideo et Cicero hos duos cursus comites solis vocavit, quia in spatio pari longe a se nunquam recedunt: luna autem tantum ab his deorsum recessit, ut quod illi anno, viginti octo diebus conficiat. Sed Cicero cum quartum de septem solem velit, quartus autem inter septem non fere medius, sed omnimodo medius et sit et habeatur, non abrupte medium solem, sed fere medium dixit his verbis: « Deinde de septem mediam fere regionem sol obtinet. » Sed non vacat adjectio qua haec pronuntiatio temperatur; nam sol quartum locum obtinens, mediam regionem tenet numero, sed non spatio; Saturni enim stella, quae summa est, Zodiacum triginta annis peragrat: sol medius anno uno; luna ultima uno mense non integro. Tantum ergo interest inter solem et Saturnum, quantum inter unum et triginta; tantum inter lunam solemque, quantum inter duodecim et unum; unde apparet totius a summo in imum spatii certam ex media parte divisionem solis regione non fieri. Sed quantum ad numerum pertinet, veluti inter septem quartus medius dicitur, quamvis propter inaequalitatem spatiorum adjectione fere particulae temperatur. Zodiacus ergo circulus est unus ex undecim supradictis, qui solus potuit latitudinem hoc modo quem referimus, adipisci. Natura coelestium circulorum incorporalis est, lineaque ita mente concipitur, ut sola longitudine censeatur, latum habere non possit; in Zodiaco longitudinem signorum capacitas exigebat. Quantum igitur spatii lata dimensio porrectis sideribus occupat, duabus lineis limitatum est, et tertia ducta per medium ecliptica vocatur, quia cum cursum suum in eadem linea pariter sol et luna conficiunt, alterius eorum necesse est evenire defectum; solis, si ei tunc luna succedat; lunae, si tunc adversa sit soli. Ideo nec sol unquam deficit, nisi cum tricesimus lunae dies est; et nisi quinto decimo cursus sui die, nescit luna defectum: sic enim evenit ut aut lunae contra solem positae, ad mutuandum ab eo solidum lumen, sub eadem linea inventus terrae conus obsistat, aut soli ipsa succedens, o jectu suo ab humano aspectu lumen ejus repellat. In defectu autem sol ipse nihil patitur, sed noster fraudatur aspectus, luna vero circa proprium defectum laborat, non accipiendo solis lumen, cujus beneficio noctem colorat; quod sciens Virgilius, disciplinarum omnium peritissimus, ait: Defectus solis varios, lunaeque labores. Quamvis igitur trium linearum ductus zodiacum et claudat et dividat, unum tamen circum auctor vocabulorum dici voluit antiquitas, secundum vero quosdam philosophos latitudo zodiaci duodecim lineis mensuratur, ex quibus juxta paris numeri naturam duas haberi medias necesse est, quas tantummodo a sole lustrari confirmantes, lunam per omnes discurrere dicunt. Quapropter ultro citroque vagata eclipsim fieri singulis mensibus non sinit. Omnibus tamen annis utriusque sideris defectus statutis diebus horisque evenire comprobant, quamvis non semper appareant, ideo quia aliquando fiunt subtus terram in parte latentis hemisphaerii, aliquando supra; sed propter nubila et propter globositatem et convexitatem terrae neque ubique, neque eisdem horis ab omnibus cerni possunt; unde certissimum est saepius ista fieri quam videri, nec aequaliter cunctis apparere cum videntur; unde vespertinos solis ac lunae defectus Orientales non sentiunt, neque matutinos Occidentales, obstante cono terrae atque visum arcente. Lunae autem defectum aliquando quinto mense a priori, solis vero septimo ejusdem bis in triginta diebus super terras occuliari, necnon ab aliis visum esse, quondam in duodecim diebus utrumque sidus deficere probabili ratione et traditione cognovimus.

Respondi ergo, ut mihi videtur, beatissime Auguste, secundum vestrarum exactionem litterarum, et dixi ex eorumdem auctoritate quemadmodum antiqui philosophi et scierunt et praescierunt, quomodo fieret defectus solis, et quando fieret illi enim omnium disciplinarum peritissimi, et nullius sectae inscii veteribus approbatae, sagacissima elimatae et defaecatae mentis intentione, et perspicacissima purgatissimaque interni sensus acie praefixa, omnium rerum naturas, rationes, causas et origines subtilissime et instantissime naturali investigatione quaesiverunt, accuratissime et efficacissime illo a quo omne datum optimum est et omne donum perfectum offerente quaesita invenerunt, inventa et deprehensa diligentissime et intentissime observaverunt inde physici astronomiae specialiter studentes, eadem diutissima meditatissimaque diligentia ortus et obitus stellarum intuentes et intuendo experientes, solis et lunae et reliquarum quinque vagantium cursus et recursus, accessus et recessus plenissime exploraverunt, in tantum ut explorando indubitatissime scirent quantas lineas zodiaci circuli unaquaeque stella erratica lustraret, et per quam proprie et specialiter de ipsis lineis in praesenti cursum dirigeret, et in quo signo et in qua parte ipsius signi esset. Qui ergo ita de subtilioribus, licet veris et naturalibus, aliarum stellarum motibus certissime et studiosissime cognoverunt, cur solis et lunae cursus, qui vere notabiliores et faciliores sunt ad cognoscendum, ignorarent, ut eos lateret quomodo vel quando per eamdem zodiaci circuli eclipticam lineam currerent, et illam unam eamdemque lustrantes, in unum signum et in unam partem coirent, et in eamdem partem coeuntes, lunaque in ipsa soli succedente eclipsis fieret solis.

Non solum ergo praedicti philosophi eclipsim, hoc est defectum solis praesciebant, et praescientes praedicebant quando post unum mensem futurus esset; sed quando per annum, aut XX aut C M annos sequeretur, per supradictam sagacem explorationem et diligentem observationem longe ante experti praesignabant. Sed ut plus miremini, usque ad quindecim millia annorum talibus argumentis protenderunt. Inde Cicero visionem Africani referens, ita dicit: « Homines populariter annum tantummodo solis unius astri reditum metiuntur; re autem recta cum ad idem unde semel profecta sunt, cuncta astra redierunt, eademque totius coeli descriptionem longis intervallis retulerunt: tunc ille vere vertens annus appellari potest, in quo vix dicere audeo quam multa hominum saecula teneantur. Namque ut olim deficere sol hominibus exstinguique visus est, cum Romuli animus haec ipsa in templa penetravit, quandoque ab eadem parte sol eodemque tempore iterum defecerit, tum signis omnibus ad idem principium stellisque revocatis, expletum annum habeto; cujus quidem anni nondum vicesimam partem scito esse conversam. »

Quae verba Tullii Ambrosiana expressio aperit hoc modo atque pandit: Annus non is solus est quem nunc communis omnium usus appellat; sed singulorum seu luminum, hoc est solis et lunae, sive stellarum, emenso omni coeli circuitu, a certo loco in eumdem locum reditus, annus suus est: sic mensis lunae annus est intra quem coeli ambitum lustrat: nam et a luna mensis dicitur, quia Graeco nomine luna μήνη vocatur.

Virgilius denique ad discretionem lunaris anni, qui brevis est, annum, qui cursu solis efficitur, significare volens ait: Interea magnum sol circumvolvitur annum. Annum magnum vocans solis comparatione lunaris; nam cursus quidem Veneris atque Mercurii pene par solis; Martis vero annus fere biennium tenet: tanto enim tempore coelum circuit. Jovis autem stella duodecim, et Saturni triginta annos in eadem circumitione consumit.

Haec de sole et luna, ac vagis, ut ante retulimus, jam nota sunt: annus vero, qui mundanus vocatur, qui vere vertens est, quia conversione plenae universitatis efficitur, largissimis saeculis explicatur, cujus ratio talis est. Stellae omnes et sidera, quae infixa coelo videntur, quorum proprium motum nunquam visus humanus sentire vel deprehendere potest, moventur tamen, et praeter coeli volubilitatem qua semper trahuntur, suo quoque accessu tam sero promovent, ut nullius hominum vita tam longa sit, quae observatione continua factam de loco per mutationem, in quo [...] primum viderat, deprehendat. Mundani ergo anni finis est, cum stellae omnes omniaque sidera, quae aplanes habet, a certo loco ad eumdem locum ita remeaverint, ut ne una quidem coeli stella in alio loco sit quam in quo fuit, cum omnes aliae ex eo loco motae sunt ad quem reversae, anno suo finem dederunt, ita ut sol et luna cum erraticis quinque in iisdem locis et partibus sint, in quibus incipiente mundano anno fuerunt: hoc autem, ut physici volunt, post annorum quindecim millia peracta contingit.

Ergo sicut annus lunae mensis est, et annus solis duodecim menses, et aliarum stellarum hi sunt anni quos supra retulimus; ita mundanum annum quindecim millia annorum, quales nunc computamus efficiunt. Ille ergo vere annus vertens vocandus est, quem non solis, id est unius astri, reditus metitur, sed quem stellarum omnium, quae in quocunque coelo sunt, ad eumdem locum reditus sub eadem coeli totius descriptione concludit; unde mundanus dicitur, quia mundus proprie coelum vocatur. Igitur sicut annum solis non solum a Kalendis Januariis usque ad easdem vocamus, sed et a sequente post Kalendas die usque ad eumdem diem, et a quocunque cujuslibet mensis die usque in diem eumdem reditus, annus vocatur; ita hujus mundani anni initium sibi quisque facit quodcunque decreverit, ut ecce nunc Cicero a defectu solis, qui sub Romuli fine contigit, mundani anni principium sibi ipse constituit, et licet etiam saepissime postea defectus solis evenerit, non dicitur tamen mundanum annum repetita defectio solis implesse, sed tunc implebitur cum sol deficiens in iisdem locis et partibus et ipse erit, et omnes coeli stellas omniaque sidera rursus inveniet in quibus fuerant sub Romulo, cum post annorum quindecim millia sicut asserunt philosophi, sol denuo ita deficiet, ut in eodem signo eademque parte sit, ad idem principium, in quo sub Romulo fuerant, stellis quoque omnibus signisque revocatis.

Anno ergo praeterito 810 ab incarnatione Domini non est mirum eclipsin solis evenisse, sicut vestrae indicant litterae; septimo Idus Junias, prima tunc initiante luna, et rursus in eodem anno pridie Kalendas Decembris, trigesima incipiente luna, et a priore defectu septimo mense, hoc est Decembre inchoante; qui sic defectus solis definitur novissima primave luna fieri, et septimo mense a priore defectu, quamvis aliquando penitus non appareat, cum certe sit factus, aut si apparuerit non semper ubique cernatur, aut si ubique conspiciatur, non eisdem horis omnes aequaliter videant evenisse propter supradictas causas.

Si quis ergo etiam in hoc tempore tanto sensus acumine praeditus, tanta instantiae diuturnitate nisus, tanta explorationis et observationis diligentia intentus, eadem otiositate et curiositate sicut priori aetate geniti, sollicitus tantum studium erga astronomiae aut cujuscunque disciplinae assectationem adhibuerit, nonne idem facile credendus est ad eamdem antiquorum scientiam et praescientiam posse pervenire? Voluntas enim dispar, non natura, quae una et aequalis est, homines tantum a se distare facit, quanquam in primis hominibus propter mundi adolescentiam et vim corporum, et sensuum vigorem magis voluisse comperimus.

Hic ergo nunc de eclipsi solis sit finis dicendi, non quod dixisse forsitan sufficienter arbitrer, sed quia ad praesens proprii ingenioli exiguitas amplius memorare non quiverit: Plinius enim secundus et alii libri, per quos aestimem haec me posse supplere, non habentur nobiscum in his partibus, cum de talibus per me ipsum nihil audeam excogitare neque praesumam. Vos autem, domine piissime Auguste, quibus prae omnibus affluentiam sapientiae, sicut et caeterarum sanctarum virtutum Deus distribuit, rogo suppliciter ut in quo vobis de hac causa ignorare videar, aut aliter aestimare quam rectum est, instruere et dirigere dignemini: Stulta enim mundi elegit Deus: Et, Non est apud eum personarum acceptio, ut non solum vestrae purissimae et clarissimae sapientiae lux his qui prope sunt luceat, sed et his qui longe; et non solum per aperta camporum discurrentes illustret, verum etiam Reclusos licet per rimas et juncturas vestri serenissimi splendoris radius exerens perfundat. Omnibus ergo valde necesse est attentis et assiduis precibus rogare et postulare, ut Dominus et Salvator noster Jesus Christus suo populo donet et tribuat multis annis de tali et tanto principe et magistro gaudere, qui omnibus aequaliter omnium bonorum operum et virtutum et honestarum disciplinarum doctor praecipuus, et perfectum habetur exemplar rectoribus ad suos subjectos bene regendos, militibus ad suam exercendam legitime militiam, clericis ad universalis Christianae religionis ritum recte observandum, philosophis et scholasticis ad honeste de humanis philosophandum et sapiendum, reverenterque atque orthodoxe de divinis sentiendum et credendum. Quid plura de nostri domini Augusti Caroli summis virtutibus et excellentibus dicere nitor, cum licet multum elaborare velim totas referre non potero? Hoc tantum veraciter dicimus, quod omnes uno ore conclamant, quia in ista terra, in qua nunc Deo donante Franci dominantur, ab initio mundi talis rex et talis princeps nunquam visus est, qui sic esset fortis, sapiens, et religiosus sicut noster dominus Augustus Carolus. De caetero autem per sua sancta et sublimia merita, forsitan de suo semine talis oriatur. Hoc solum superest ut nos omnes Christiani altissimis vocibus et devotissimis cordibus unanimiter clamemus ad Dominum et rogemus ut nostri optimi domini Augusti Caroli triumphos multiplicet, imperium dilatet, sacram conservet progeniem, sanitatem confirmet, vitam in multos extendat annorum curriculos. Exaudi, exaudi, exaudi, Christe.

Sicut ergo, domine reverentissime atque dulcissime, Deo et vestro fideli famulo Waldoni abbati mandastis, ut me de talibus ex vestris verbis commonendo interrogaret, et exigendo commoneret, qui sicut vobis fidelis, ita mihi de hac re gravis et importunus exactor quamvis moderate exstitit, ita per illum vobis remitto, ut inde ei gratias referatis, si quid in his bene dixerim, quae per ejus urgentem exactionem volens nolens solvi: si autem aliquid male propter meum proprium neglectum, mihi poenitentiam quam velitis clementer imponatis. Opto vos bene semper valere in Deo, optime domine, et non tantum optime domine, sed et piissime atque amantissime Pater.

This work was produced in association with:

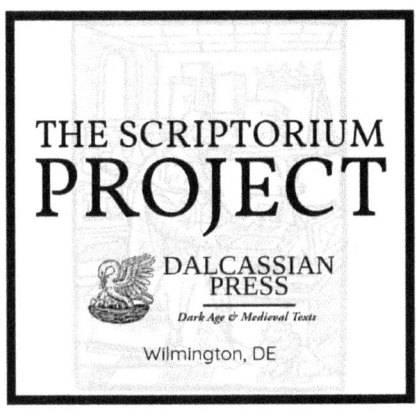

www.ingramcontent.com/pod-product-compliance
Lightning Source LLC
LaVergne TN
LVHW061049070526
838201LV00074B/5237